JAPAN NATIONAL SOCCER TEAMS

ULTIMATE FAN GUIDE

DAVID STABLER

Lerner Publications ◆ Minneapolis

Lerner Publications Company
An imprint of Lerner Publishing Group, Inc.
241 First Avenue North
Minneapolis, MN 55401 USA

For reading levels and more information, look up this title at www.lernerbooks.com.

Main body text set in Aptifer Slab LT Pro.
Typeface provided by Linotype AG.

Editor: Matt Doeden **Designer:** Viet Chu **Photo Editor:** Elena Mai

Library of Congress Cataloging-in-Publication Data

Names: Stabler, David author
Title: Japan national soccer teams : ultimate fan guide / David Stabler.
Other titles: Ultimate fan guide
Description: Minneapolis : Lerner Publications, [2026] | Series: Lerner Sports. World Cup fan guides | Includes bibliographical references and index. | Audience: Ages 7–11 | Audience: Grades 4–6 | Summary: "Soccer has long been popular in Japan, but the country has only recently become a soccer powerhouse. Learn about the growth of the men's team and how the women's team became one of the world's best"— Provided by publisher.
Identifiers: LCCN 2025011856 (print) | LCCN 2025011857 (ebook) | ISBN 9798765689424 lib. bdg. | ISBN 9798348029340 pbk | ISBN 9798765698785 epub
Subjects: LCSH: World Cup (Soccer) | Soccer teams—Japan—History—21st century—Juvenile literature | LCGFT: Literature.
Classification: LCC GV943.6.G36 S83 2026 (print) | LCC GV943.6.G36 (ebook) | DDC 796.334/6680952—dc23/eng/20250626

LC record available at https://lccn.loc.gov/2025011856
LC ebook record available at https://lccn.loc.gov/2025011857

Manufactured in the United States of America
1-1012740-54810-8/11/2025

TABLE OF CONTENTS

Saki Kumagai (*background*) scores the winning goal in the 2011 Women's World Cup.

INTRODUCTION

JAPAN RISING

The tension was high in Frankfurt, Germany. It was the 2011 Women's World Cup final. Japan and the United States were locked in a close game. The country of Japan had been hit by a terrible earthquake and tsunami earlier that year. Its players wanted to win to inspire hope for their nation.

The United States struck first when forward Alex Morgan fired a powerful shot into the net. Then, with just minutes left in the game, Japan tied the score. The game went into extra time.

Abby Wambach's header gave the United States a 2–1 lead. But Japan refused to give up. With only three minutes remaining, team captain Homare Sawa delivered a goal off a corner kick, tying the game at 2–2. The match came down to penalty kicks.

Japan took a 2–1 lead in the penalty kicks. Saki Kumagai, a young player for Japan, walked to take the next shot with a chance to win it. She took a deep breath. She kicked. The ball flew past the goalkeeper. Goal!

FAST FACTS

The Japanese women's team was the first Asian team to win the Women's World Cup.

The Japanese women's team is known as Nadeshiko Japan, or Pink Japan.

The Japanese men's soccer team came back to win after trailing Sweden 2–0 in the 1936 Olympics.

The Japanese soccer teams' mascot is a black crow named Yatagarasu.

Goalkeeper Ayumi Kaihori dives to make a save in a 2011 World Cup match.

Japan was the World Cup champion. The players jumped and hugged. Tears streamed down their faces. The crowd cheered and waved Japanese flags.

The men's and women's national teams are made up of the best players in Japan. They face off against other national teams in some of the biggest soccer tournaments in the world. The Men's World Cup and Women's World Cup are the biggest prizes. But the teams also fight for glory in the Olympic Games, the Asian Cup, and more.

Japan's players cheer as they celebrate their 2011 World Cup title.

Kunishige Kamamoto kicks the ball past Mexico's goalkeeper at the 1968 Olympics. Japan won the match to claim the bronze medal.

CHAPTER 1

BUILDING THE FOUNDATIONS

Soccer in Japan has a long and exciting history. In the 1870s, a British naval officer taught some Japanese students how to play the game. The students loved it. Soon, more and more people started playing soccer in Japan.

In 1921, the Japan Football Association (JFA) was formed. This group helped grow the sport in the country. The JFA started a national tournament called the Emperor's Cup, which is still played today. The JFA's symbol, a three-legged crow called Yatagarasu, became the mascot of the Japanese national soccer team.

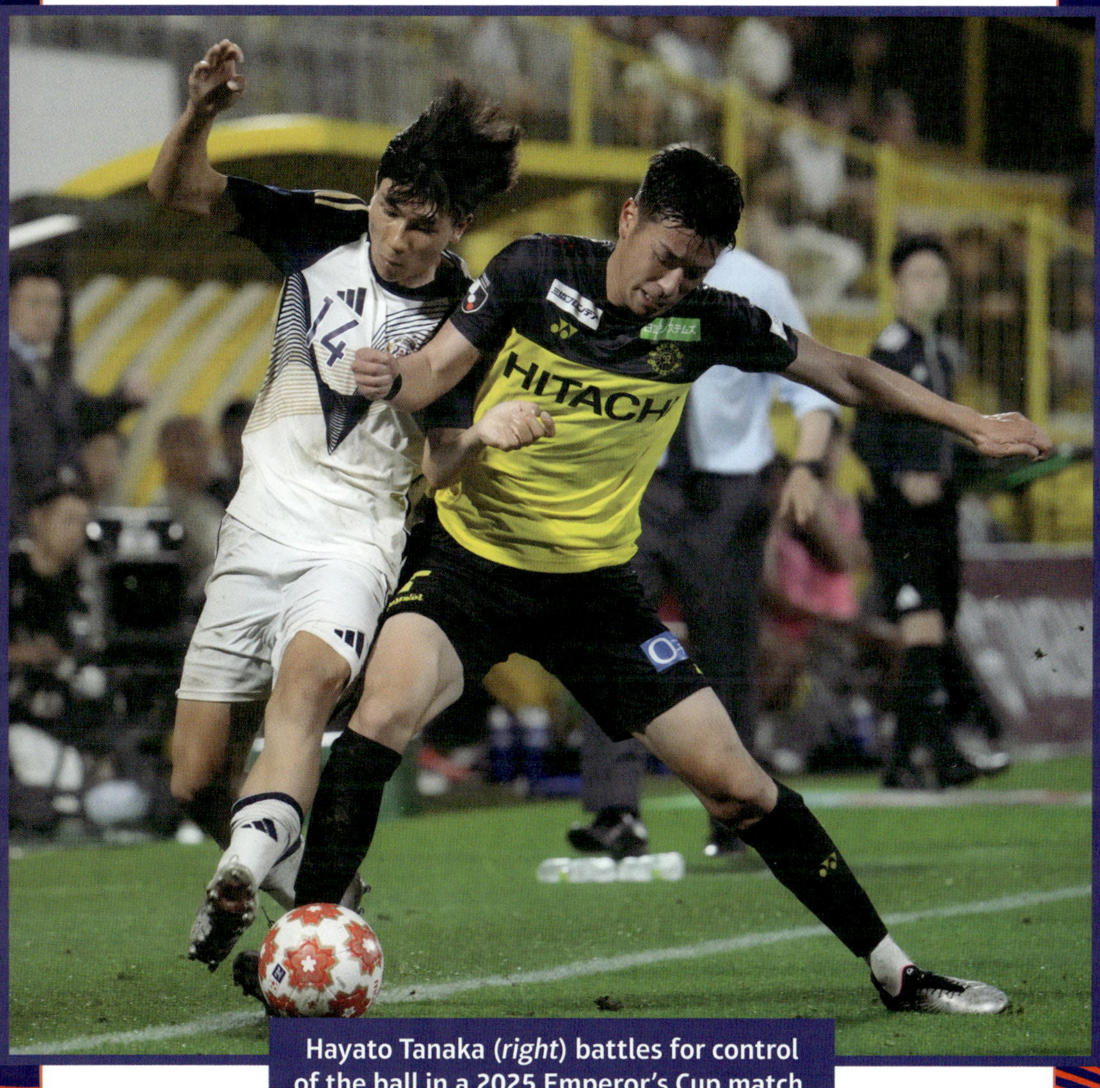

Hayato Tanaka (*right*) battles for control of the ball in a 2025 Emperor's Cup match.

In the 1920s, Japan played in the Far Eastern Championship Games, competing against teams from China and the Philippines. In 1936, Japan's men's team made the Olympic Games for the first time. They fell behind 2–0 to Sweden in their first game. But they came back to win, 3–2. The team was getting better and better.

That progress was cut off by the outbreak of World War II (1939–1945). After the war ended, soccer in Japan began to recover. The Emperor's Cup resumed in 1946. This marked the beginning of the sport's revival in the country.

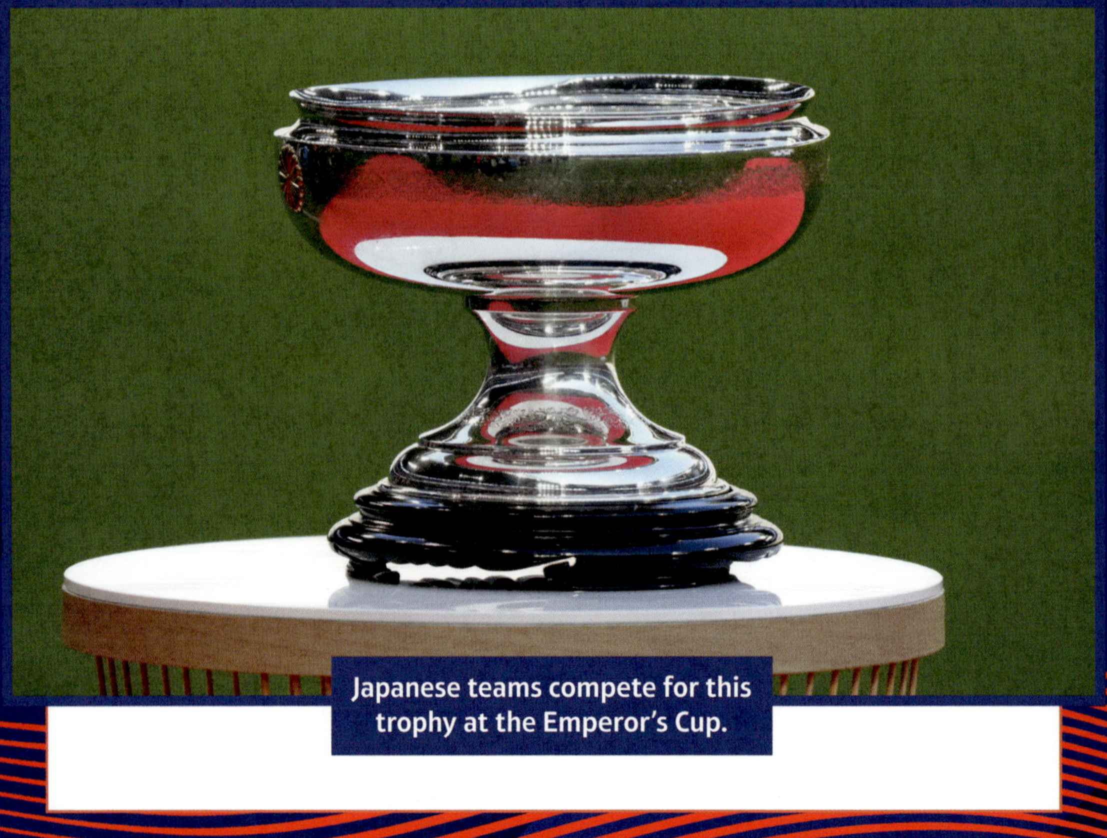

Japanese teams compete for this trophy at the Emperor's Cup.

Mao Hosoya (*left*) is a star on Japan's national team. Here, he battles Yasuki Kimoto during a club match.

For many years, there were no pro soccer players in Japan. Players had to work regular jobs while competing. But everything changed in 1992 with the launch of the J-League, Japan's first pro soccer league. With more training, better coaching, and strong support from fans, Japan's men's national team grew stronger. They became one of Asia's top teams, regularly competing in the World Cup and winning the Asian Cup.

Men's soccer in Japan had been growing for decades. But women's soccer took longer to develop. In the 1970s, more people around the world became interested in women's soccer. Japan formed its women's national team in 1981.

At first, it wasn't easy. The women's team struggled with low funding and little attention from the media. Many players had to balance soccer with full-time jobs.

Nahomi Kawasumi (*left*) chases down a loose ball in a 2011 World Cup match.

Mizuho Sakaguchi is on the attack during the 2011 World Cup.

But Japan's women's team kept building. Over the years, they gained more support and began competing in major tournaments. Their hard work paid off in 2011. They made history by beating the United States to win the World Cup. It was a moment of pride for the nation, proving that Japan was a force in women's soccer.

DAWN OF A NEW DAY

The first girls' soccer team in Japan was formed at an elementary school in the city of Kobe in 1966.

Japan launched the WE League in 2021. It was Asia's first pro women's soccer league. It gave young Japanese women the chance to dream of becoming pro soccer players one day.

Thanks to decades of dedication, Japan has become a true soccer powerhouse. Both the men's and women's teams continue to shine on the world stage. They inspire future players and prove that Japan belongs among the best in global soccer.

The WE League team Sanfrecce Hiroshima Regina celebrates winning the 2023 WE League Cup title.

Tomokazu Myojin (*right*) collides with Tugay Kerimoğlu of Turkey in a 2002 World Cup match.

CHAPTER 2

SUPER MOMENTS

The men's team, known as the Samurai Blue, made history in 1998 by qualifying for their first World Cup. Since then, Japan has qualified for every World Cup. One of their biggest moments came in 2002 when Japan cohosted the World Cup with South Korea. The team reached the round

Junya Ito leaps over the leg of a Croatian defender at the 2022 World Cup.

of 16. They repeated this feat in 2010, 2018, and 2022. Fans enjoyed their fast-paced style of play and strong sense of teamwork.

Japan has produced some legendary men's players. Kazuyoshi Miura, known as King Kazu, was one of the country's first soccer superstars. He still plays for club teams in his 50s! Miura's incredible longevity is an inspiration to older players. In 2025, he was still playing at the age of 58.

BLOND AMBITION

Hidetoshi Nakata dyed his dark hair blond for the 1998 World Cup. He hoped it would make him stand out and get noticed by pro teams in Europe.

Other players have taken on leadership roles as King Kazu has gotten older. Hidetoshi Nakata was a midfielder who helped Japan succeed in the early 2000s. He was known for his quick feet, dribbling skills, and fashion sense. Keisuke Honda was famous for his powerful free kicks and leadership. Shinji Kagawa was a pinpoint passer whose two goals in the 2011 Asian Cup quarterfinals against Qatar helped Japan secure a 3–2 victory.

Midfielder Hidetoshi Nakata starred for the national team in the early 2000s.

Japan's women's national team, known as Nadeshiko Japan, or Pink Japan, made history in 2011 by winning the Women's World Cup. The success didn't stop there. In 2012, they won a silver medal at the London Olympics. In 2015, the women reached the World Cup final again. Though they finished in second place, their performances proved they were one of the world's best teams.

Japan's women's soccer legends include Homare Sawa. She won the Ballon d'Or in 2011 as the world's best player.

Japan and the United States battle at the 2015 World Cup.

Homare Sawa (*right*) leads the charge in a 2008 Olympic match against the United States.

She led Japan to World Cup glory and scored 83 goals for the women's team, making her the country's all-time leading scorer.

As a young player, Sawa had few options to play soccer. After elementary school, there weren't many teams for girls. She often had to play on boys' teams. When Sawa finally found a women's team to play on, many of her teammates were much older than her. This age gap made it difficult for her to compete. Sawa overcame these challenges and became one of the best soccer players in the world.

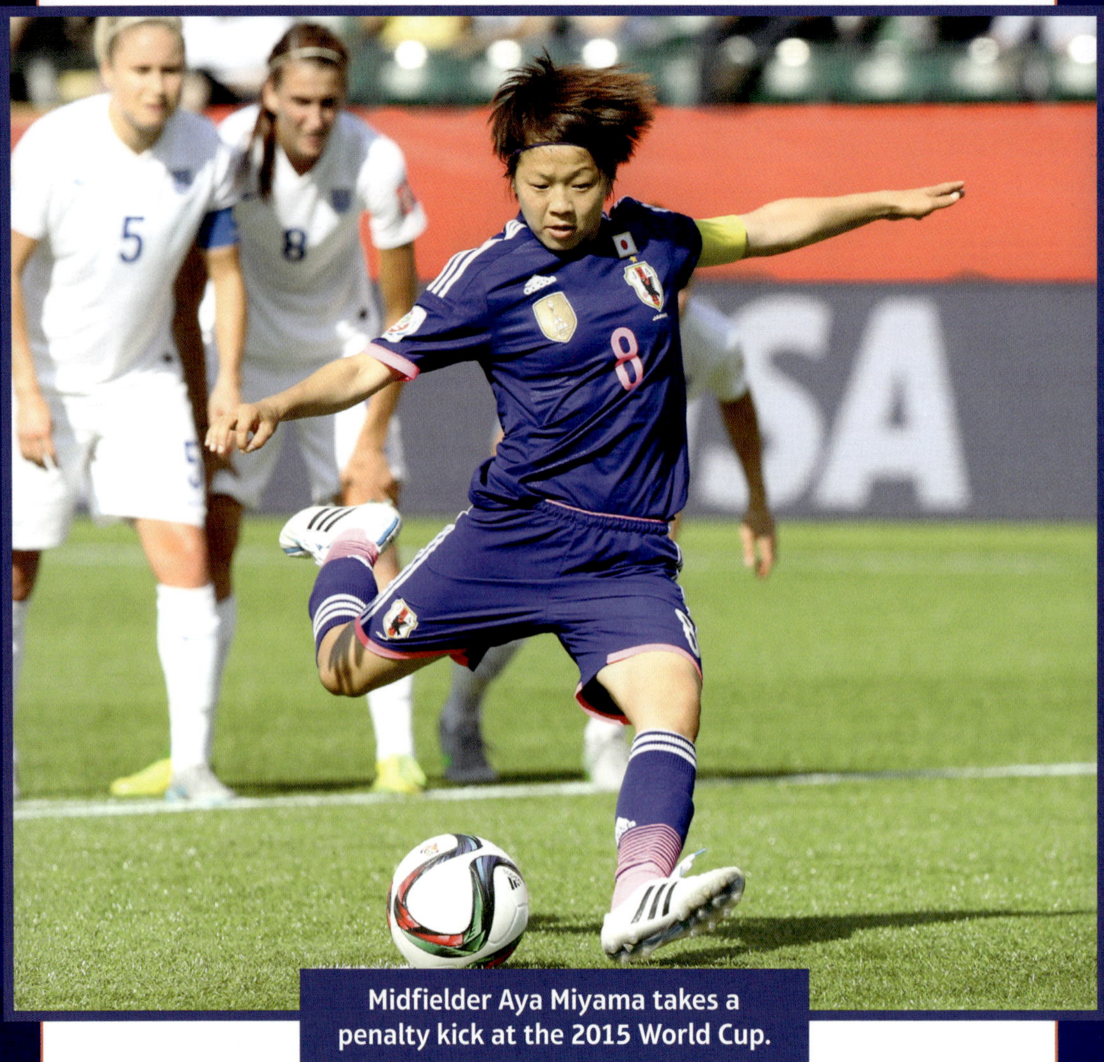

Midfielder Aya Miyama takes a penalty kick at the 2015 World Cup.

Aya Miyama, known for her passing and leadership, was a key player in Japan's rise to World Cup glory. Mana Iwabuchi, a talented forward, won the World Cup at the age of 18. Iwabuchi continued to lead the Japanese women's team until her retirement in 2023 at the age of 30.

Japan fans proudly wave flags at a 2023 match against Turkey.

CHAPTER 3

PASSIONATE FANS, BRIGHT FUTURE

Though baseball has long been Japan's favorite sport, soccer is growing more and more popular. People of all ages love to watch and play the game. The Japanese national teams have made their country proud on the world stage. But soccer in Japan is about more than just winning. It brings people together around a shared passion for the game.

Japanese fans celebrate a 2025 victory in a Men's World Cup qualifying match.

Japanese soccer fans are some of the best in the world. Both the men's and women's teams have loyal supporters who cheer them on with colorful banners and chants. No matter the result, Japanese fans always show good sportsmanship.

CLEANUP TIME

Japanese soccer fans are famous for their tidiness. They have been cleaning up the stands after World Cup matches since Japan first played in the tournament in 1998.

So how did soccer get so popular in Japan? *Captain Tsubasa*, a popular manga comic book series, helped ignite the country's soccer boom in the 1980s. Its hero, Tsubasa Oozora, is an 11-year-old Japanese boy who dreams of winning the World Cup.

Captain Tsubasa, a popular manga character in Japan, helped ignite interest in soccer.

The series taught basic soccer skills to a large audience in Japan. It inspired young people to take up the sport. Many pro players, including Hidetoshi Nakata, credit *Captain Tsubasa* with sparking their interest in soccer.

The influence of *Captain Tsubasa* lives on. It has inspired the creation of more soccer-related manga. The popular stories contribute to Sakka Cultcha, or Soccer Culture, in Japan.

Hidetoshi Nakata takes a shot in a 1997 World Cup qualifying match.

Zion Suzuki controls the ball for Japan at a World Cup qualifying match in 2025.

Soccer is also important in schools and communities. Many kids play the game in school clubs, and programs help young players develop their skills. The JFA works to grow the sport, making sure more boys and girls have a chance to play.

Japan's men's team has improved a lot over the years. They have played in every World Cup since 1998. With the 2026 Men's World Cup coming soon, Japan is aiming for its best performance yet. Center Ko Itakura and goalkeeper Zion Suzuki are two of the young players to watch as Japan heads into the tournament.

Defender Toko Koga boots a crossing pass at the 2025 SheBelieves Cup.

Since the women's team won the World Cup in 2011, women's soccer in Japan has become much more popular. The WE League, Japan's pro women's soccer league, is helping more players compete at a high level. Japan has invested a lot of money and resources into women's soccer, and it has paid off.

In 2025, rising stars Toko Koga, Mina Tanaka, and Yuka Momiki led the Japanese women to an upset win over the United States in the final of the SheBelieves Cup, an international tournament. With strong leadership and new talent, the future looks bright for Nadeshiko Japan.

Japanese soccer is on the rise. It has become a big part of Japanese culture and national pride. With talented players, strong teamwork, and a love for the game, Japan's future is full of excitement.

Forward Mina Tanaka is on the attack at the 2024 Olympics.

JAPAN MEN'S SOCCER TIMELINE

1917 Japan plays its first international match against China.

1992 The team captures its first Asian Cup title.

1998 Japan qualifies for the World Cup for the first time.

2000 Japan secures its second Asian Cup victory.

2002 Japan cohosts the World Cup with South Korea, advancing to the round of 16.

2004 The team claims its third Asian Cup championship.

2011 Japan wins its fourth Asian Cup.

2022 Japan advances to the round of 16 in the World Cup again.

JAPAN WOMEN'S SOCCER TIMELINE

1981 Japan plays its first international match.

1991 The team qualifies for the first Women's World Cup.

2011 Japan becomes the first Asian team to win the Women's World Cup.

2012 The team earns a silver medal at the London Olympics.

2015 Japan finishes as runners-up in the Women's World Cup.

2018 Japan wins the AFC Women's Asian Cup for the second time.

2023 The team participates in its ninth straight Women's World Cup.

2025 Japan beats the United States to win the SheBelieves Cup.

GLOSSARY

Ballon d'Or: a prize given every year to the best soccer player in the world

club team: a pro soccer team

corner kick: a free kick from a corner of a soccer field

forward: an attacking player whose primary role is to score goals

goalkeeper: the player who stands in front of the goal and tries to stop the other team from scoring

manga: a type of comic popular in Japan

mascot: a person, animal, or object used as a symbol to represent a sports team

midfielder: a player who plays mostly in the middle of the field

penalty kick: a free shot at the goal after a foul or to decide some games

sportsmanship: when people playing or watching a sport treat others with respect

tsunami: a great sea wave produced especially by an earthquake or volcanic eruption under the sea

LEARN MORE

Kiddle: Football Facts for Kids
https://kids.kiddle.co/Football

Kiddle: Football in Japan Facts For Kids
https://kids.kiddle.co/Football_in_Japan

Scheff, Matt. *The World Cup: Soccer's Greatest Tournament*. Lerner Publications, 2021.

Science Kids: Fun Soccer Facts for Kids
https://www.sciencekids.co.nz/sciencefacts/sports/soccer.html

Shaw, Gina. *What Is the Women's World Cup?* Penguin Workshop, 2023.

Streeter, Anthony. *World Cup All-Time Greats*. Press Box Books, 2025.

INDEX

PHOTO ACKNOWLEDGMENTS

Image credits: AP Photo/Frank Augstein, p. 4; Mike Hewitt/FIFA via Getty Images, p. 6; AP Photo/Michael Sohn, p. 7; The Asahi Shimbun via Getty Images, p. 8; Hiroki Watanabe/Getty Images, p. 9; Etsuo Hara/Getty Images, p. 10; YUTAKA/AFLO SPORT/Alamy, p. 11; Jonathan Paul Larsen/Diadem Images/Alamy, p. 12; Friedemann Vogel/Getty Images, p. 13; Kyodo via AP Images, p. 14; Stu Forster/Getty Images, p. 15; Press Association via AP Images, p. 16; Allstar Picture Library Ltd/Alamy, p. 17; Vaughn Ridley/PA Images/Alamy, p. 18; Aflo Editorial/Alamy, p. 19; The Yomiuri Shimbun via AP Image, p. 20; D .Nakashima/AFLO/Alamy, p. 21, 25; AP Photo/Eugene Hoshiko, p. 22; Imaginechina/Alamy, p. 23; AP Photo/Mike Fiala, p. 24; Jon Endow/Image of Sport/Alamy, p. 26; Nippon News/Naoki Morita/AFLO SPORT/Alamy, p. 27; Design elements: Ralf Hiemisch/Getty Images; Rifqyhsn Design/Getty Images; cunfek/Getty Images; poo worawit/Getty Images.

Cover: MATSUO K/AFLO SPORT/Alamy (left); YUTAKA/AFLO SPORT/Alamy (right).